# Queenisms

## 101 *Jolts* of Inspiration

Kathy Kinney and Cindy Ratzlaff

# DEDICATION

To our Mothers, sisters, daughters and friends, glorious women all.

# A NOTE TO OUR READERS

Little did we know when we wrote *Queen of Your Own Life* that our book would be the beginning of a new journey for us and the tens of thousands of women who decided to go on that journey with us. We have been humbled and honored to find so many new friends through Facebook, Twitter and at live events across the country.

What we've discovered in talking with these amazing women is a powerful hunger for community; a longing for a place to go where you can always find connection, support and inspiration. So we began posting Queenisms™ on Facebook and our website – vintage inspired graphics with a short positive messages.

We both lead very busy lives, as is true for every woman we know. For us, an image and a few positive words is a quick and easy way to change the direction of our day. These Queenisms have helped us to discover new solutions to old problems – like getting an invaluable bit of advice from a true and trusted friend. They have also helped us to understand that not only are we not alone but we are all more alike than different. We hope Queenisms can be the same for you.

You can read the book straight through or open to any page randomly. It's your decision. Each page is a self-contained thought or meditation. We'd love to invite you to join us for more daily *jolts* of inspiration on Facebook at Queen of Your Own Life.

Mostly, we want you to know that happiness is a choice. You get to decide everyday how you want to live your day. Sometimes a *jolt* of inspiration is all you need to help you make the choice to be happy. Life doesn't have to be so hard.

Royally yours,

Kathy Kinney and Cindy Ratzlaff

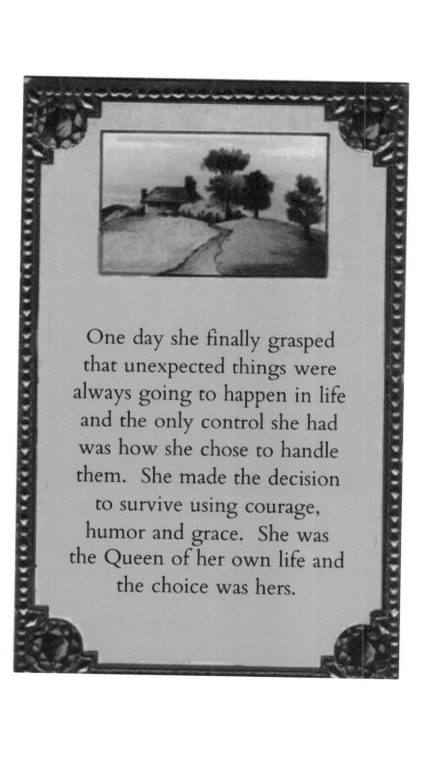

One day she finally grasped
that unexpected things were
always going to happen in life
and the only control she had
was how she chose to handle
them. She made the decision
to survive using courage,
humor and grace. She was
the Queen of her own life and
the choice was hers.

She needed to stop thinking of her life with fear.
Instead, she decided to see it for what it was.
A bold adventure being led by a
very brave woman.

It really wasn't any of her business
what anyone thought of her.

So she decided she was going to be herself.

She was a thoroughly modern woman with
one old-fashioned quality - gumption.
She had all the gumption necessary to survive
anything life might bring her way.

She really admired that about herself.

She decided that whenever life felt wild and
dangerous, she would throw her head back,
fling her arms up in the air, find her balance and
dare to enjoy the ride

# POST CARD

Dear Me,

You are beautiful. You are intelligent. You are creative. You are valuable. In short, you are perfect just the way you are. I love you and I will always have your back.

Love, Me

She was the only one who could make herself
Queen of her own life.

So she did.

It felt very good to be Queen.

The fact is there is not a limited amount of
happiness in the world.  So all she had to do
to have some in her life, was to understand that
she was just as worthy as everyone else.

She needed a reminder from someone who
loved her very much that she was doing
a really good job of living life.

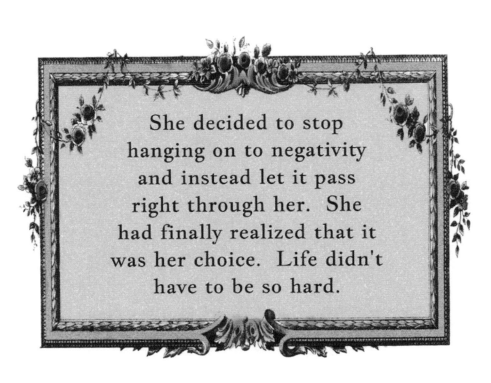

She decided to stop
hanging on to negativity
and instead let it pass
right through her.  She
had finally realized that it
was her choice.  Life didn't
have to be so hard.

# COURAGE

More than anything she was tired of being afraid.

So she decided to let go of the past, not worry about the future and live only in the now.

She had the courage to build a happy life for herself.

She was thirsty, but not for water.
What she wanted was a big drink of life.

She realized that saying yes to everyone else
meant saying no to herself.

She decided to nip it in the bud.

Be kind to yourself because you are worthy of your own admiration.

Change was not only a natural part of life,
it was the only way to reveal the true beauty within.

She looked in the mirror and said,
"I love you and I will take better care of you."

The time to start loving herself was now.

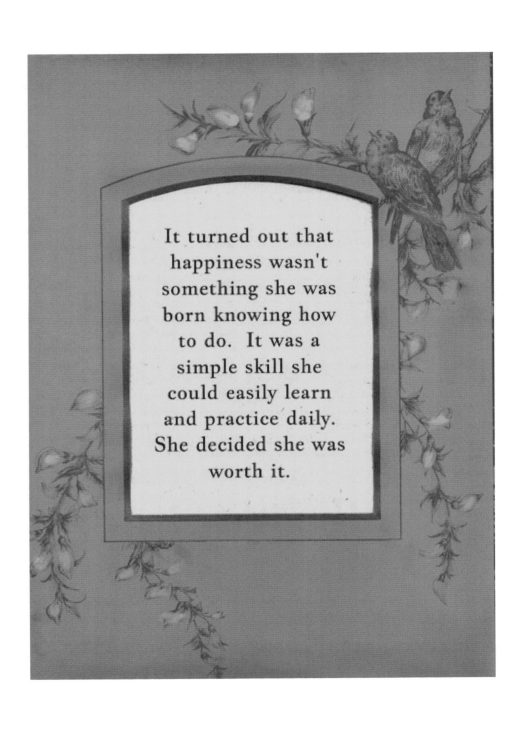

It turned out that happiness wasn't something she was born knowing how to do. It was a simple skill she could easily learn and practice daily. She decided she was worth it.

She would walk slowly and steadily through her fear.
She knew it was better to try than
to never have tried at all.

She would look for all of the funny moments in her life.
When she found them she would give
herself the gift of enjoying them.

She simply decided to have more fun because she deserved it.

There was no right or wrong way to live life.
She could only fail if she let
fear get in the way.

The practice of happiness is best done in
the company of supportive, agenda free friends.

When she emerged from her cocoon,
she realized the transformation
had been worth the struggle.

She knew if she could get her mind in shape,
her body would follow.

Somewhere along the journey she simply forgot how amazing she was. She vowed to never forget again.

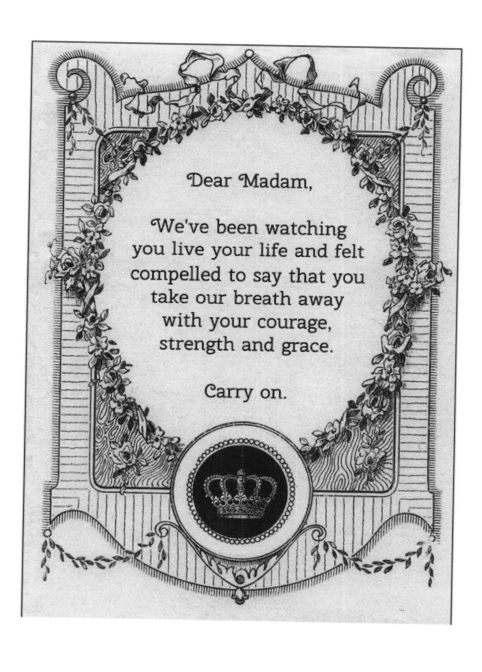

Dear Madam,

We've been watching
you live your life and felt
compelled to say that you
take our breath away
with your courage,
strength and grace.

Carry on.

Can you meet me next
Tuesday for lunch?

She spent the day enjoying her own company.
She decided to make a date with herself more often.

One day she was complaining, yet again, that her life was making her crazy.

Her friend said, "Wasn't it Einstein who said the definition of insanity is doing the same thing over and over and expecting different results?

She decided Einstein and her friend were very smart. It was time to open herself up to finding a new way to balance and happiness.

She was done being a whiner.
She decided it was time to be a winner.

A Woman Of Her Word

Yes means yes
and
No means no

She was getting good at setting strong boundaries

.

She decided to show everyone how to treat her by taking very good care of herself.

If she didn't set the example, who would?

She decided the old quote, "It's never too late to have
a happy childhood," was going to be true for her.
It was a gift she could give herself
and she deserved it.

She wanted to say thank you
for the kindness and the encouragement.
So she bought herself some flowers.

Dear Madam,

It has come to our attention that you do not clearly see that you are quite a marvelous woman. It has also been reported that you, on occasion, speak ill of yourself.

You are hereby asked to cease and desist.


Best Regards,
Your Queen Voice

She had been
looking at the negative
side of her life for so long that she
had become the worst kind of
Queen - a Drama Queen.
So, she decided to let go of the
drama and begin the
practice of being
happy.

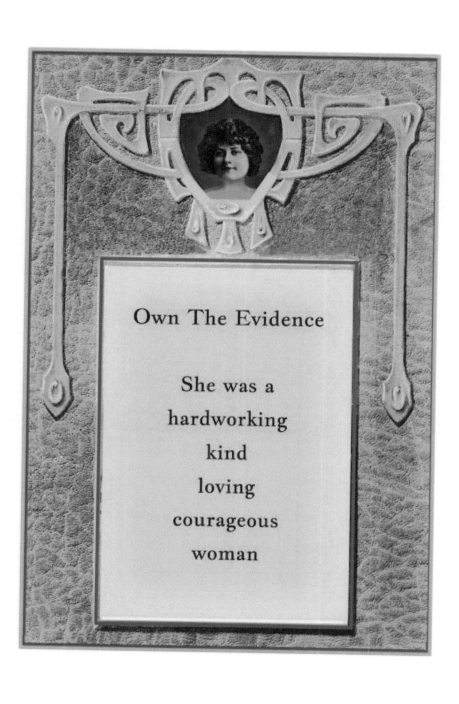

Own The Evidence

She was a
hardworking
kind
loving
courageous
woman

She taped a note to her mirror to remind herself
there is always something more.

She would look for
the open doors.
When she found
them she would
walk through
keeping her heart
and mind open to all
the possibilities
of success and joy
life had to offer.

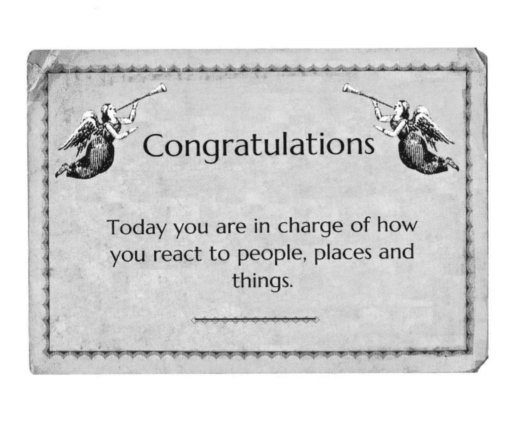

# Congratulations

Today you are in charge of how you react to people, places and things.

The only one stopping her from being who she wanted to be was her. She decided it was time to get out of her own way and live the dazzling life she was meant to live. She was the radiant Queen of her own life and her energy was strong enough to light up the whole world.

She decided she would give love abundantly all year long and she would start with herself.

She was a wonderful woman,
living an ordinary life in an extraordinary way.

Another thing she really liked about herself.

She made a deal with herself.
She wouldn't allow anyone to say
cruel and unkind things to her anymore
and she would stop talking to herself that way as well.

It was a win-win situation.

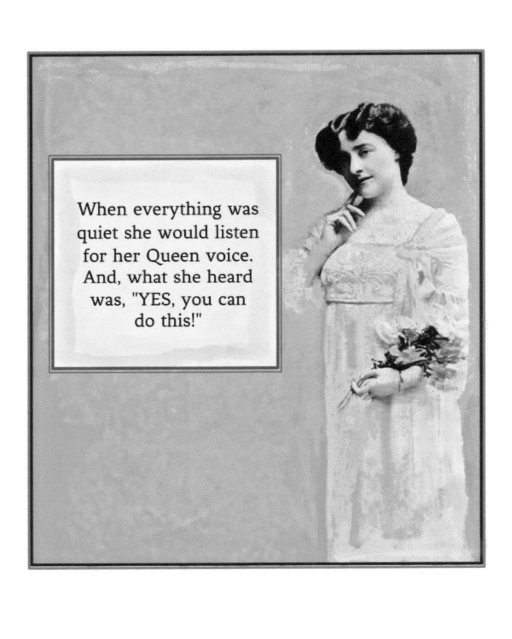

When everything was quiet she would listen for her Queen voice. And, what she heard was, "YES, you can do this!"

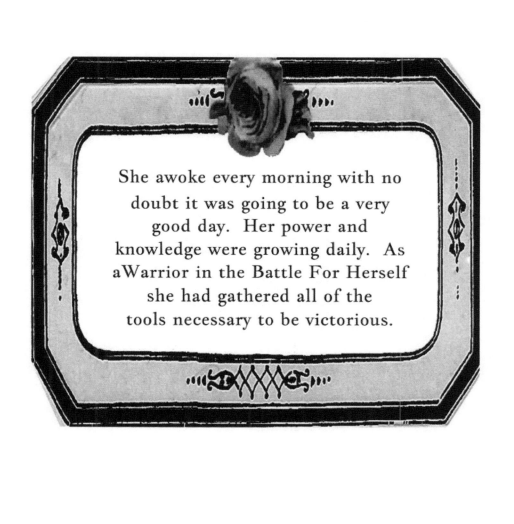

She awoke every morning with no
doubt it was going to be a very
good day.  Her power and
knowledge were growing daily.  As
a Warrior in the Battle For Herself
she had gathered all of the
tools necessary to be victorious.

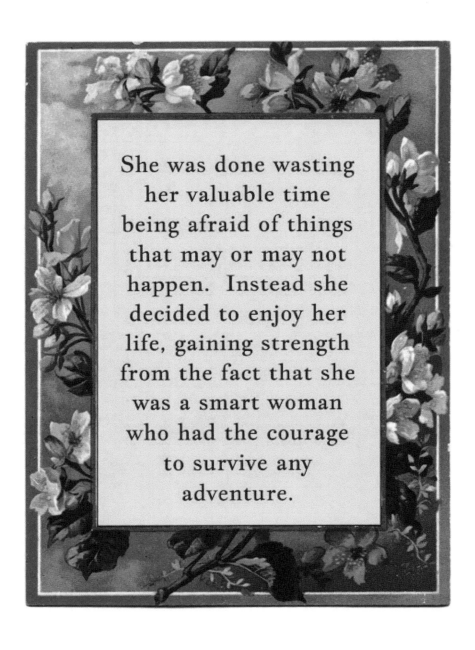

She was done wasting her valuable time being afraid of things that may or may not happen.  Instead she decided to enjoy her life, gaining strength from the fact that she was a smart woman who had the courage to survive any adventure.

It didn't matter who liked her

as long as she loved herself.

It took a lot less energy to have a positive attitude than it did to have a negative one.

And, you felt a lot better at the end of the day.

She could no longer label her experiences good or bad.

It was all just life.

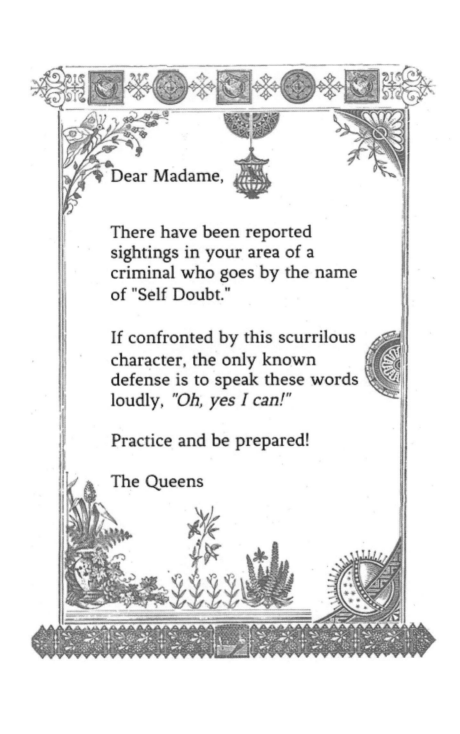

Dear Madame,

There have been reported sightings in your area of a criminal who goes by the name of "Self Doubt."

If confronted by this scurrilous character, the only known defense is to speak these words loudly, *"Oh, yes I can!"*

Practice and be prepared!

The Queens

She thought, "My time is valuable and I'm not going to waste it having hurt feelings.

No one can hurt my feelings unless I let them and I've decided I'm not going to let them.

She decided to stop beating herself up
for shortcomings only she could see.

QUEEN

For today she decided to just take a deep breath and put one foot in front of the other. She realized it was progress, and not perfection, that would get her where she wanted to go.

Your Invitation

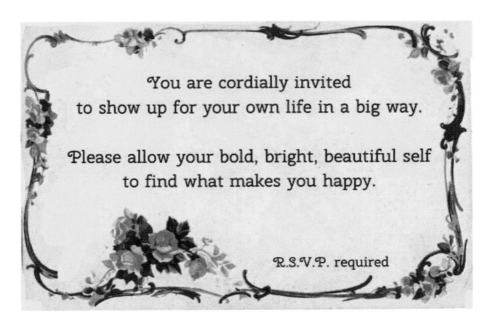

You are cordially invited
to show up for your own life in a big way.

Please allow your bold, bright, beautiful self
to find what makes you happy.

R.S.V.P. required

She was such an amazing woman,
but she was the only one who couldn't see it.

She chose to live this day as a powerful,
intelligent woman; one who had the ability
to navigate the day with grace and humor
because that's who she was.

Once she decided to see her beauty
more clearly than her flaws, she was delighted.

I believe in you.

She decided it was high time
she started believing in herself.

She decided to remind herself every morning, "This day is the beginning of a brand new adventure." She was the Queen of Her Own Life and she could choose how she wanted to live it.

It was time she realized there were many more things right in her life than wrong.

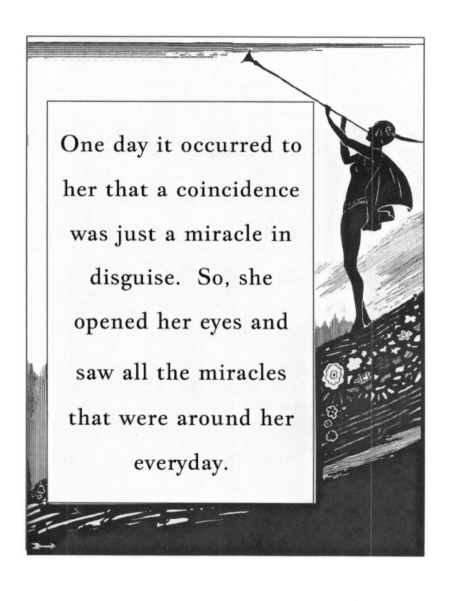

One day it occurred to
her that a coincidence
was just a miracle in
disguise.  So, she
opened her eyes and
saw all the miracles
that were around her
everyday.

She realized that in order to have a good friend,
she had to be one.

She often felt alone – even in a crowd.
So she decided to be brave
and share who she really was
That way everyone else could do the same.

She really was capable of handling
anything that came her way.

Her friends saw her as
loving, generous and
a bright light in the
world.  Since her
friends were very
intelligent, she decided
to believe them.

She was tired of not getting
what she needed, yet she
knew it was no one's fault
but her own.  So she
decided she would show the
world how to treat her by
loving herself completely
and unconditionally.  It
would take practice but she
was worth the work.

IF NOT NOW...WHEN?

QUEEN

*of your own life*

There was something worse than trying and failing.
It was having never tried at all.

**BY ORDER OF THE QUEEN**

You are hereby awarded

The Medal of Courage

…for getting out of bed everyday
and showing up with a smile.

Life had made her into a beautiful pearl.

She remembered what someone once told her,
"A little grit and a lot of pressure
make a beautiful pearl."

The only opinion of her that truly mattered
was her own.

She promised herself not to forget it again.

It's never too late to become a swan.

Life was a glorious adventure
and she was woman enough to enjoy it.

When *is* the last time you did something
for the first time?

The truth was she could have all the money in the
world and everything it could buy,
and she still wouldn't be happy.

Happiness was an inside job that required
practice and patience.

She decided she was worth the work.

She decided to gently let go of the
hurtful people in her life.

She had the courage to take care of herself.

One day
she realized that
ignoring her problems
didn't make them go away.
It just made them last
longer.  She decided to face
each problem slowly, one at a
time.  She was so
much stronger and braver
than she realized.

She decided to practice being patient with family, friends, pets and especially herself.

## Overdue Notice

Dear Madame,

Our records indicate that you have
not taken a deep breath nor
allowed yourself time to sit, dream
or relax recently.

We respectfully request that you
rectify this situation immediately.

The Queens

She believed that you get what you give.
So she decided to treat everyone
with love, kindness and respect.

She decided it was time for her
to put on her wings and fly.

She remembered feeling sassy
and full of possibilities.

She decided to find out if that little girl was still there.

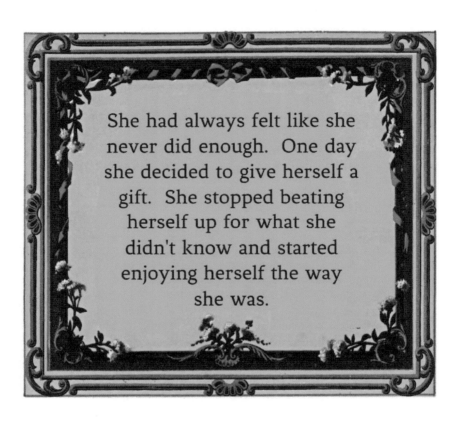

She had always felt like she never did enough. One day she decided to give herself a gift. She stopped beating herself up for what she didn't know and started enjoying herself the way she was.

She realized she was worthy of her own admiration.

All of her friends thought, "It's about time!"

She realized that life was what it was. And suddenly she understood the only part of it she had any control over was how she lived it.
So, she chose to do it with self love.

She always put everyone else's needs before her own.
She decided today would be different.
Today she would put herself first.

She was a smart woman.
So she decided to take the "ish" out of selfish.

# TO DO

Get car fixed

Buy cat litter

Stake up tomatoes

Make dinner

Do laundry

Spend time with me

She often got so caught up in being who she thought she
*should* be, that she didn't know who she was.

She decided to get out of her own way
and let her true self shine through.

She knew she felt better about herself
when she looked good.
So she decided to take better care of herself.

If she didn't, who would?

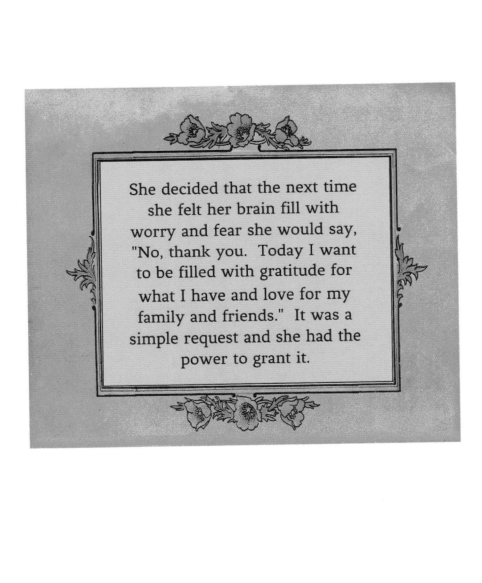

She decided that the next time she felt her brain fill with worry and fear she would say, "No, thank you. Today I want to be filled with gratitude for what I have and love for my family and friends." It was a simple request and she had the power to grant it.

She spent so much time worrying about
the bad things that might happen
that she missed enjoying the now.

She decided to just let go and enjoy the ride.

Suddenly the word
luscious came to mind
snd she decided to use
that word at least three
times today, just to make
herself smile.

She deserved to be surrounded by
loving and supportive friends.

As befitted a woman who was Queen of her own life,
she decided to live today with love, humor and grace.

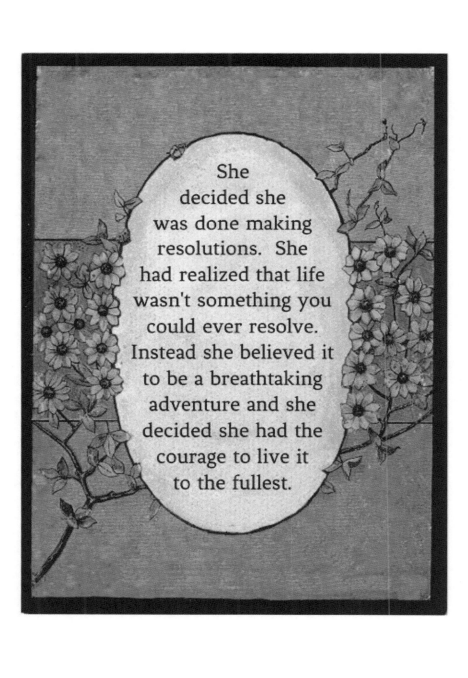

She
decided she
was done making
resolutions.  She
had realized that life
wasn't something you
could ever resolve.
Instead she believed it
to be a breathtaking
adventure and she
decided she had the
courage to live it
to the fullest.

She finally realized she wasn't the Queen
of the whole world – only the Queen of her own life.

Her relief was enormous and she vowed to never put
that kind of pressure on herself again.

Fresh new day. Brand
new chance. She took
a breath and stepped
out into the world.

# ACKNOWLEDGEMENTS

We would like to thank Karen, the Graphics Fairy, for her amazing website of vintage, royalty free images. We highly recommend her site for crafters, bloggers and anyone who wants to be inspired to create. Her site was a great resource for gathering the elements we needed to design the images used in our book. http://graphicsfairy.blogspot.com/

Another huge thank you goes to Amy Barickman for her friendship, encouragement and for giving us permission to use several images from her delightful website The Vintage Workshop. Along with her other website, Indygo Junction, Amy's sites are filled with fun and interesting projects. http://thevintageworkshop.com and http://indygojunction.com

We are grateful to both of these women for sharing their creativity and love of vintage images.

# Also by Kathy Kinney
## and
## Cindy Ratzlaff

## Available at Amazon!

## Queen Of Your Own Life

The Grownup Woman's Guide To Claiming
Happiness and Getting the Life You Deserve

# ABOUT THE AUTHORS

**CINDY RATZLAFF** is an award winning marketing and branding professional hailed by *Forbes* as one of the "Best Branded Women on Twitter," and by *Forbes Woman* as one of the "Most Influential Women on Entrepreneurship." She is a regular contributor to BusinessInsider.com and is founder of Brand New Brand You Inc., a brand-marketing consultancy.

**KATHY KINNEY** is probably best known for her iconic role as Mimi on *The Drew Carey Show*. She has acted in over a dozen films, guest-starred on numerous television shows and has toured worldwide with Drew Carey and the Improv All-Stars. Kathy may be seen on the ABC Family hit show, *The Secret Life of the American Teenager,* as well as in the title role of Mrs. P at **www.mrsp.com**. This award winning children's website is aimed at keeping alive the joy of reading.

# CREDITS

Sources of images: When creating our visual Queenisms, we made every effort to use images which are either part of the public domain or which are not restricted by copyright. All images from Amy Barickman at The Vintage Workshop are used by her permission and all rights are reserved. We apologize for any errors or omissions and would be grateful if notified of any corrections that should be incorporated in future reprints or editions of this book.

We invite you to join the Queen community wherever you love to play. We can be found at:

Facebook: http://Facebook.com/QueenofYourOwnLife

Twitter: http://Twitter.com/QueenofOwnLife

YouTube:
http://youtube.com/QueenofYourOwnLife

Or our website:
http://QueenofYourOwnLife.com